Selected Images
original
photographs

Joseph Fleming

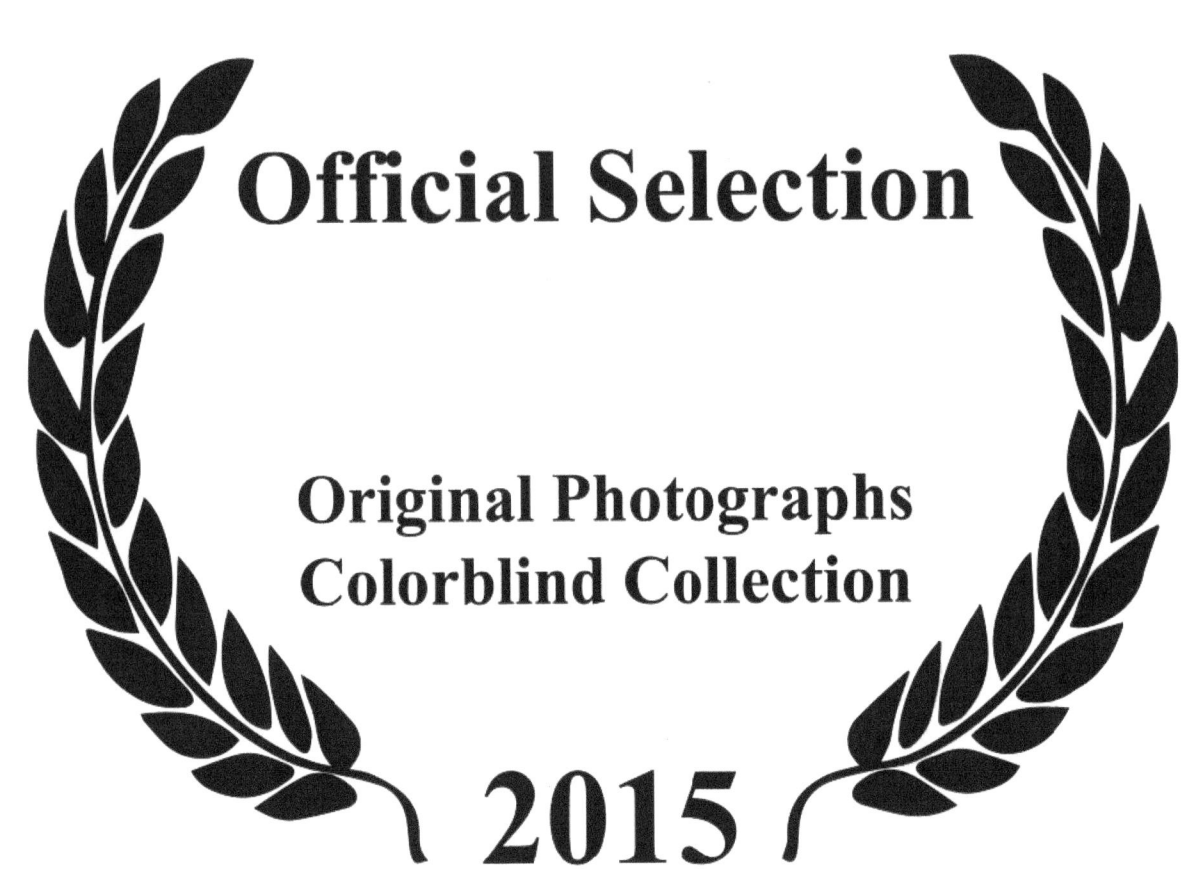

Official Selection

Original Photographs
Colorblind Collection

2015

Colorblind Black & White
photography portfolio

Decades of being around accomplished talent producing absolutely phenomenal quality work has taught that we are capable of greatness. It is possible to meet our destiny and become it. Experiencing excellence done with such apparent ease and humble selfless gratification is the motivation for this photography. Most important was having the freedom.

Being colorblind gives an advantage when composing black & white... less confusion.

These selections, from thousands of captures during years of travels, exhibit the lonely freedom of a hidden perspective. All images were framed in the camera and presented without edits, genuine as seen through the lens. Panchromatic conversion applied by unique proprietary process.

Original fine art and custom work available.

info@ BEACHNOISE.com

JOSEPH FLEMING

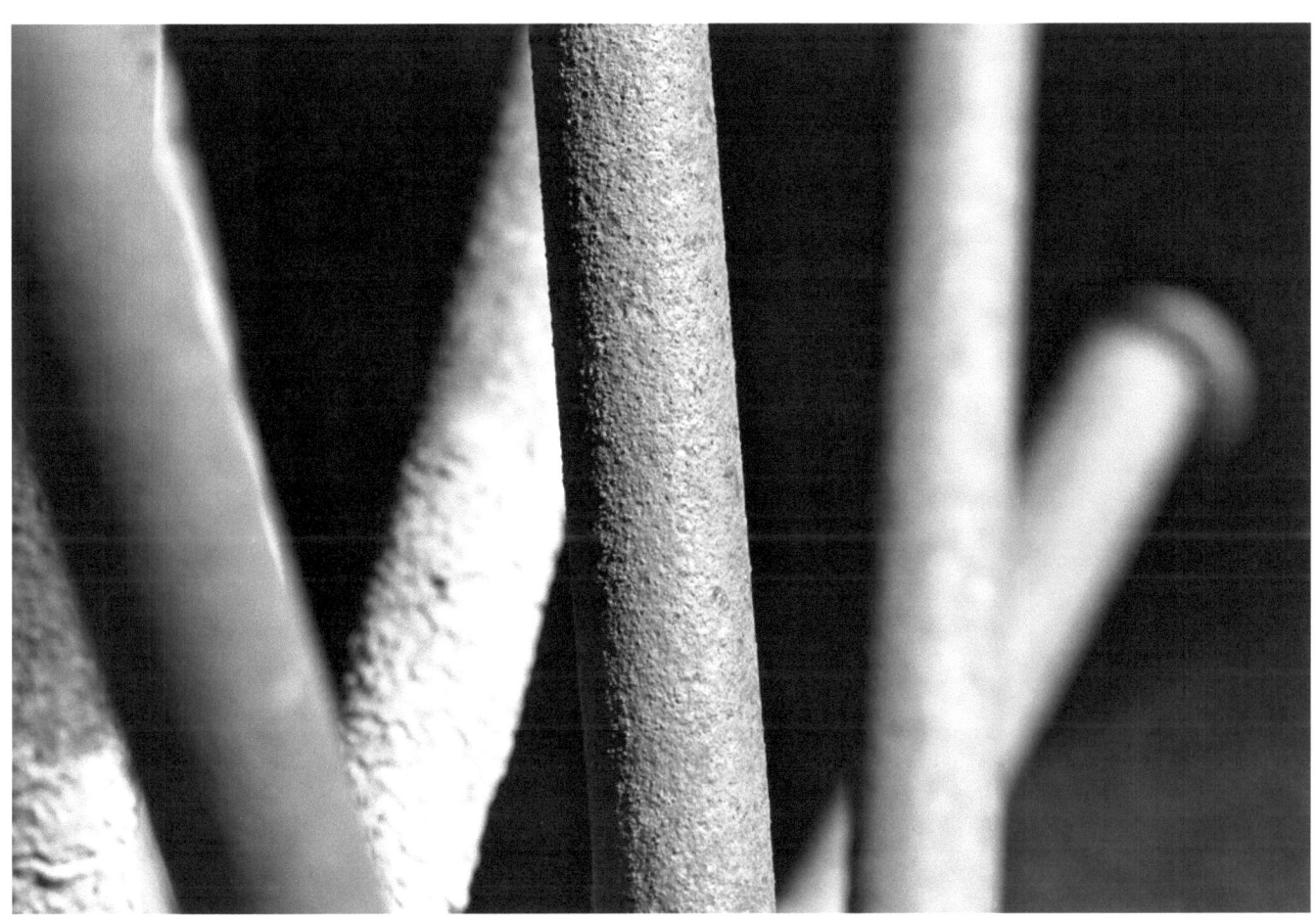

0780

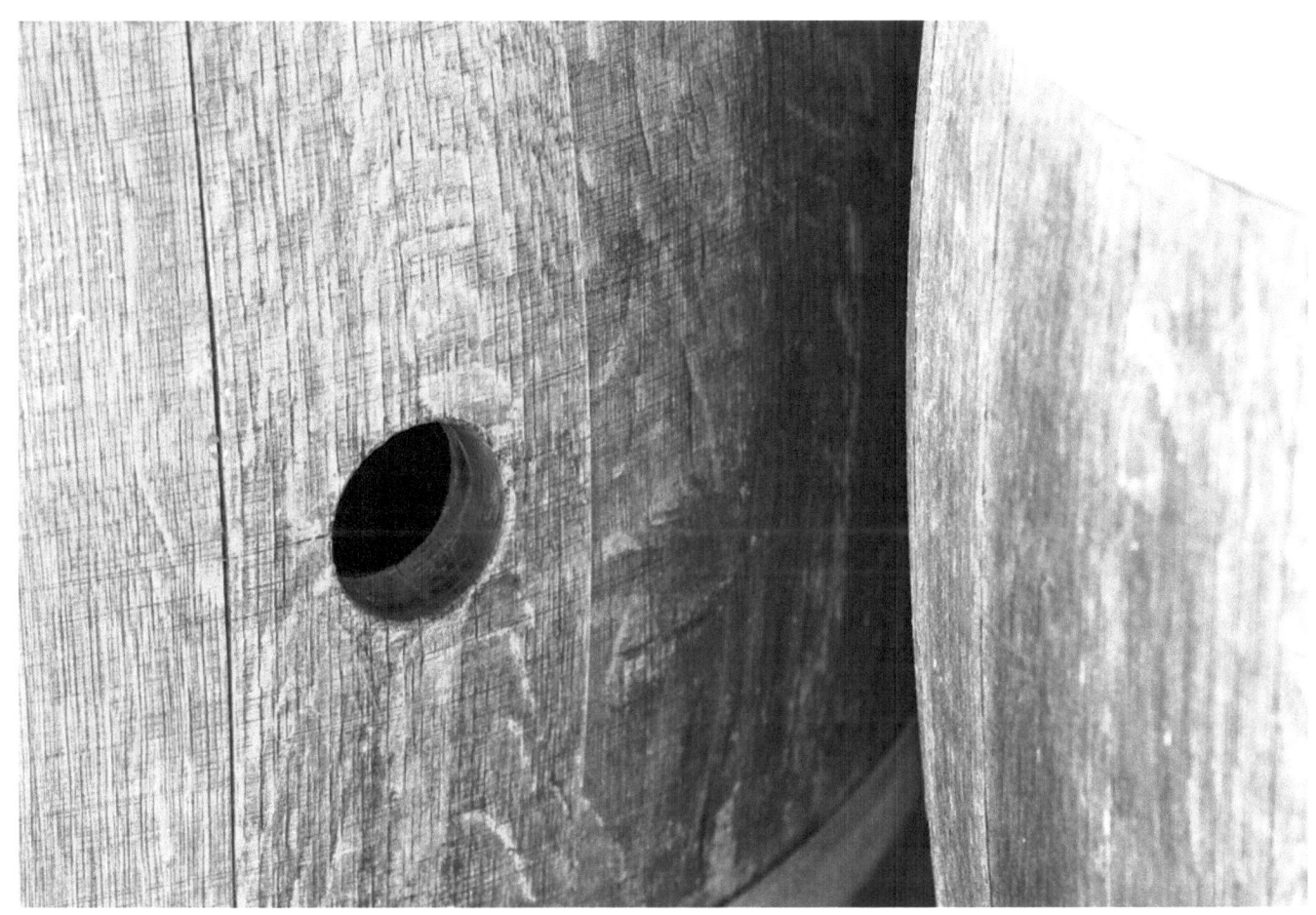

0826

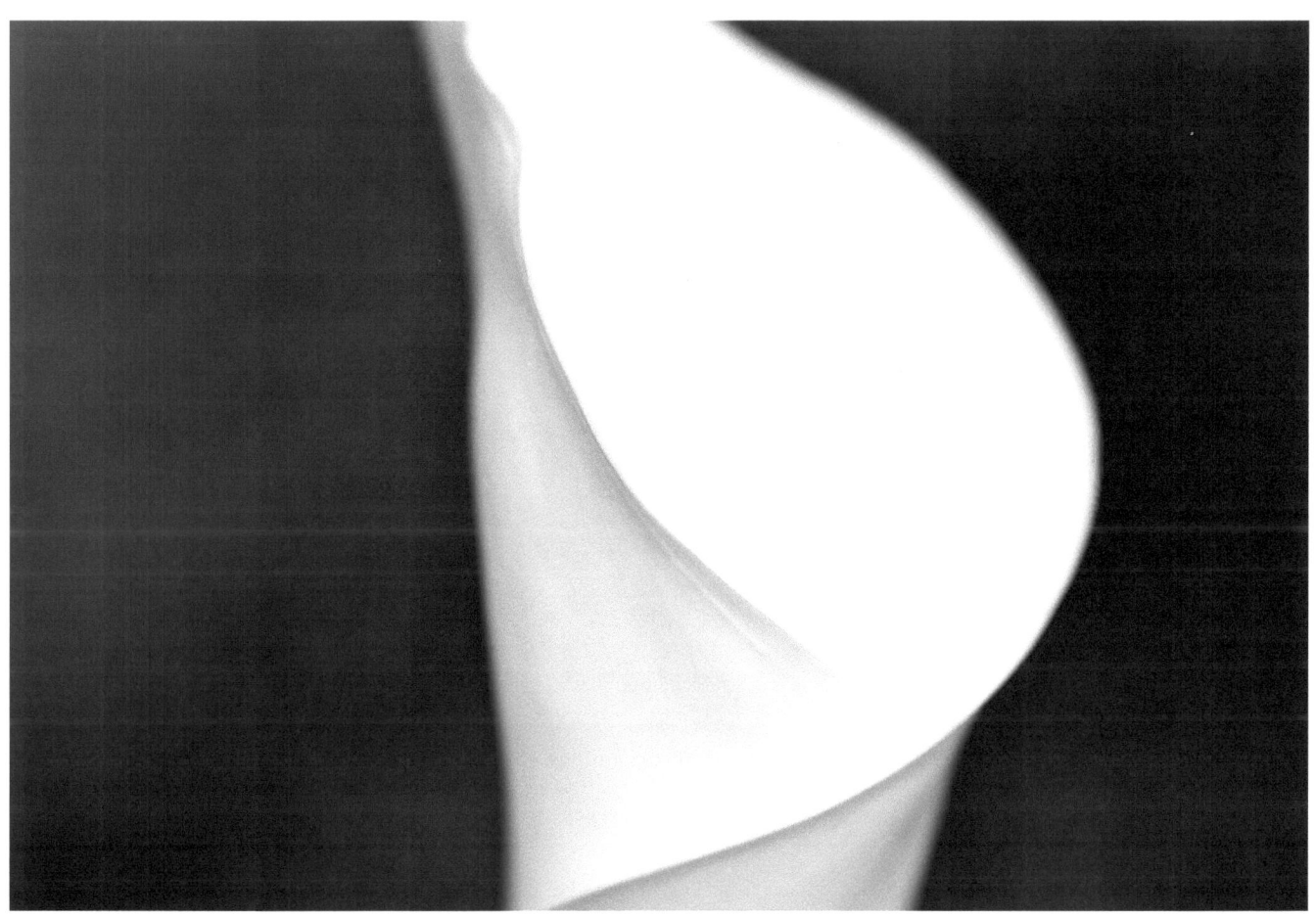

0920

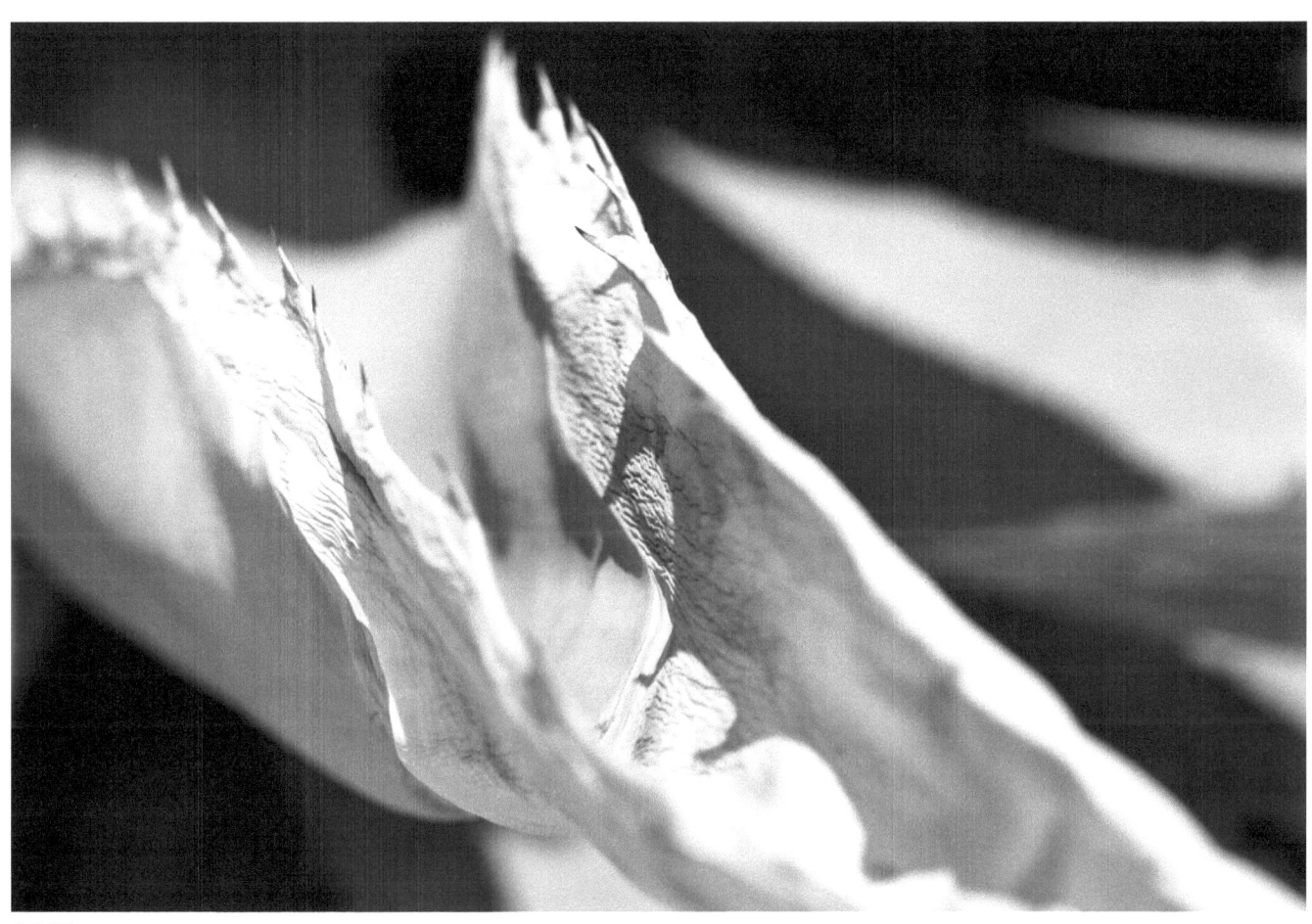

1581

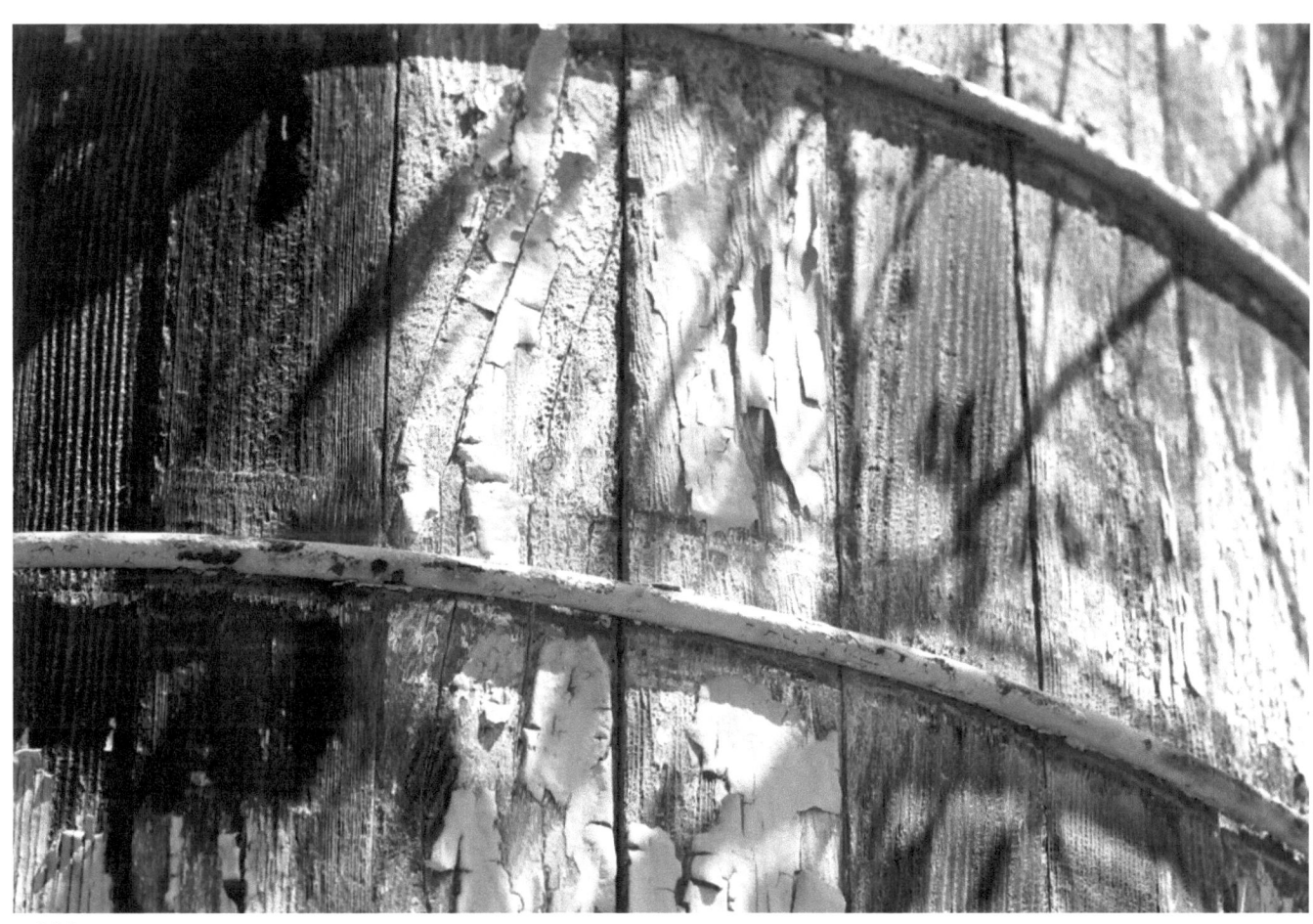

1608

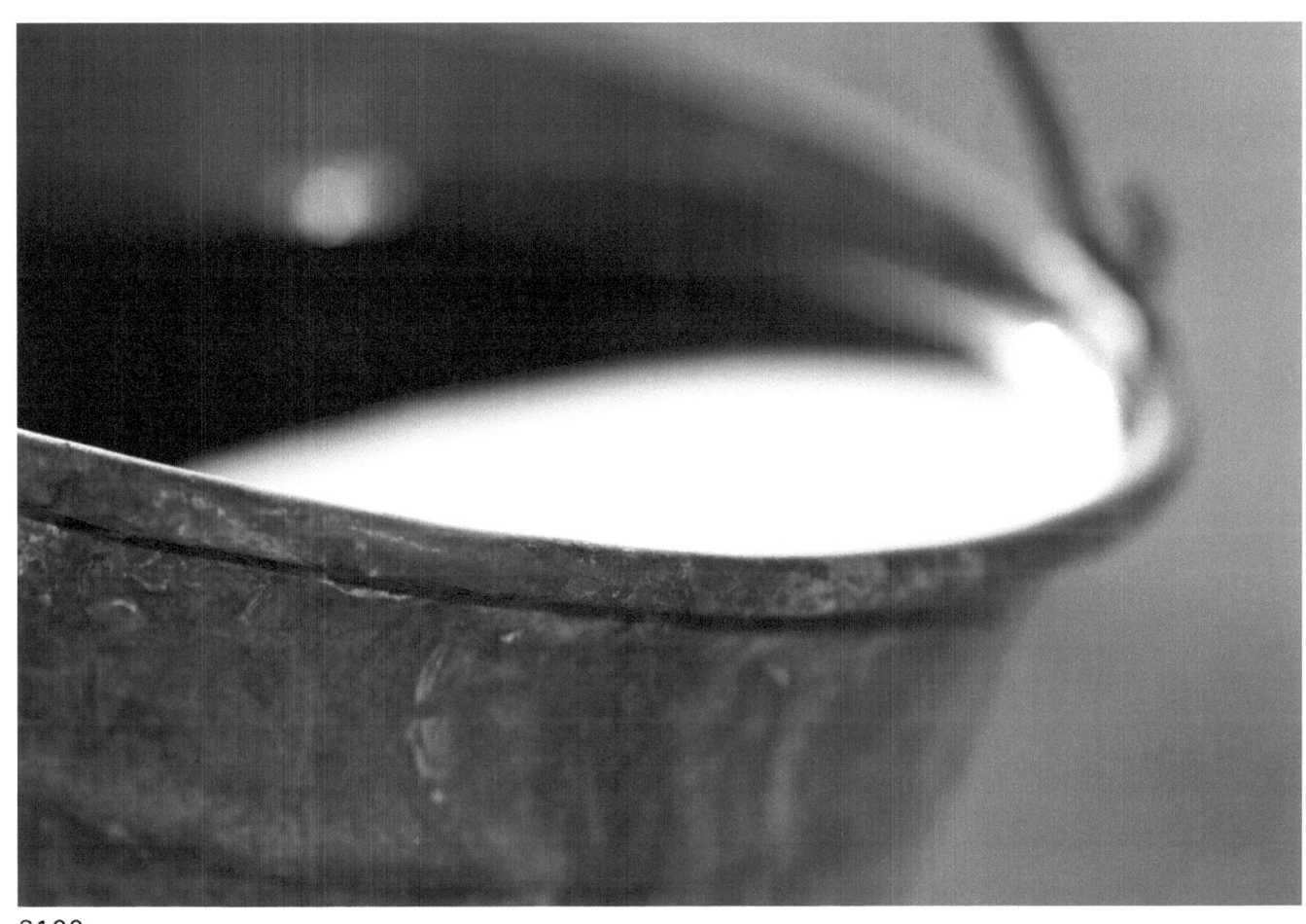

2180

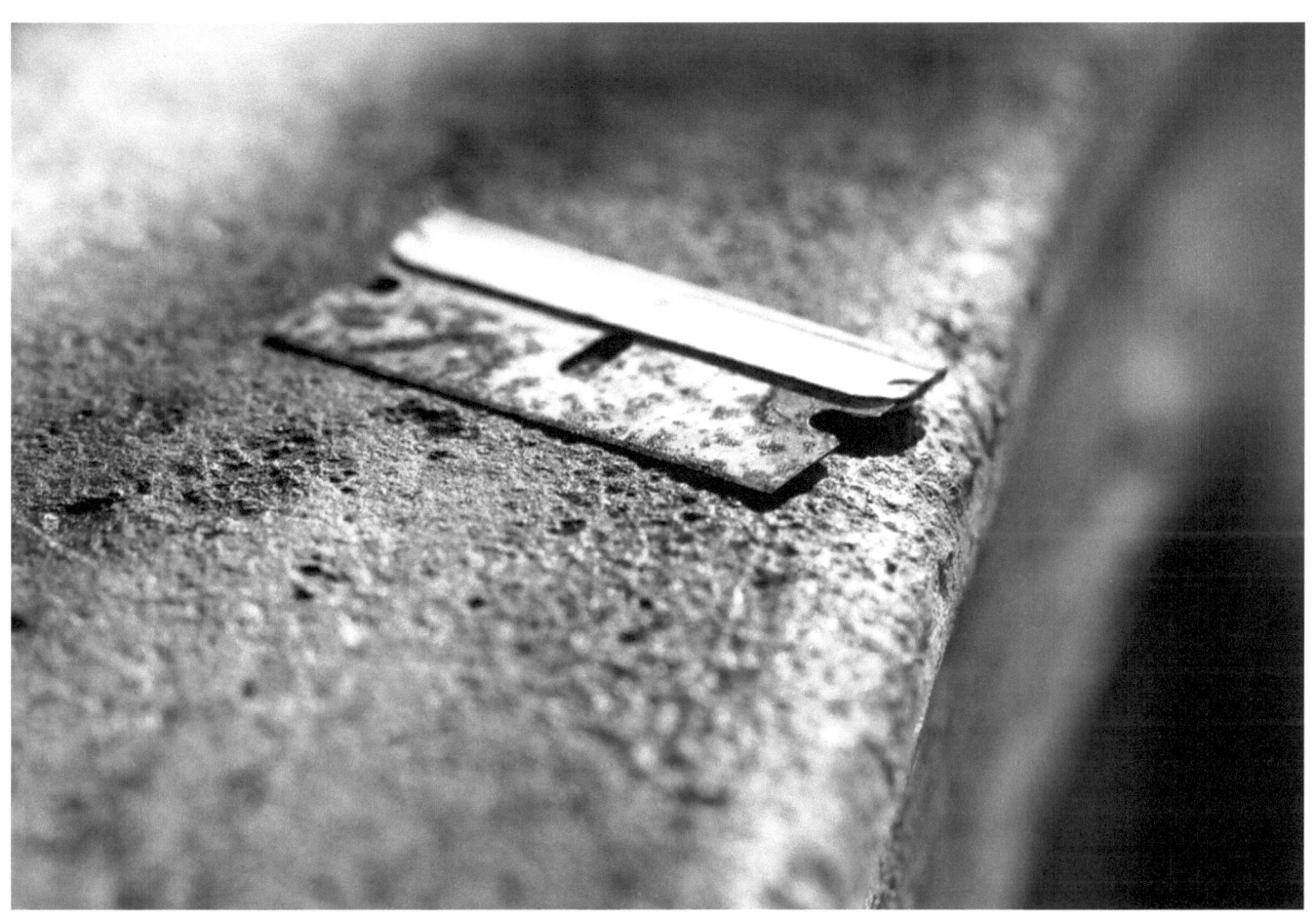

2467

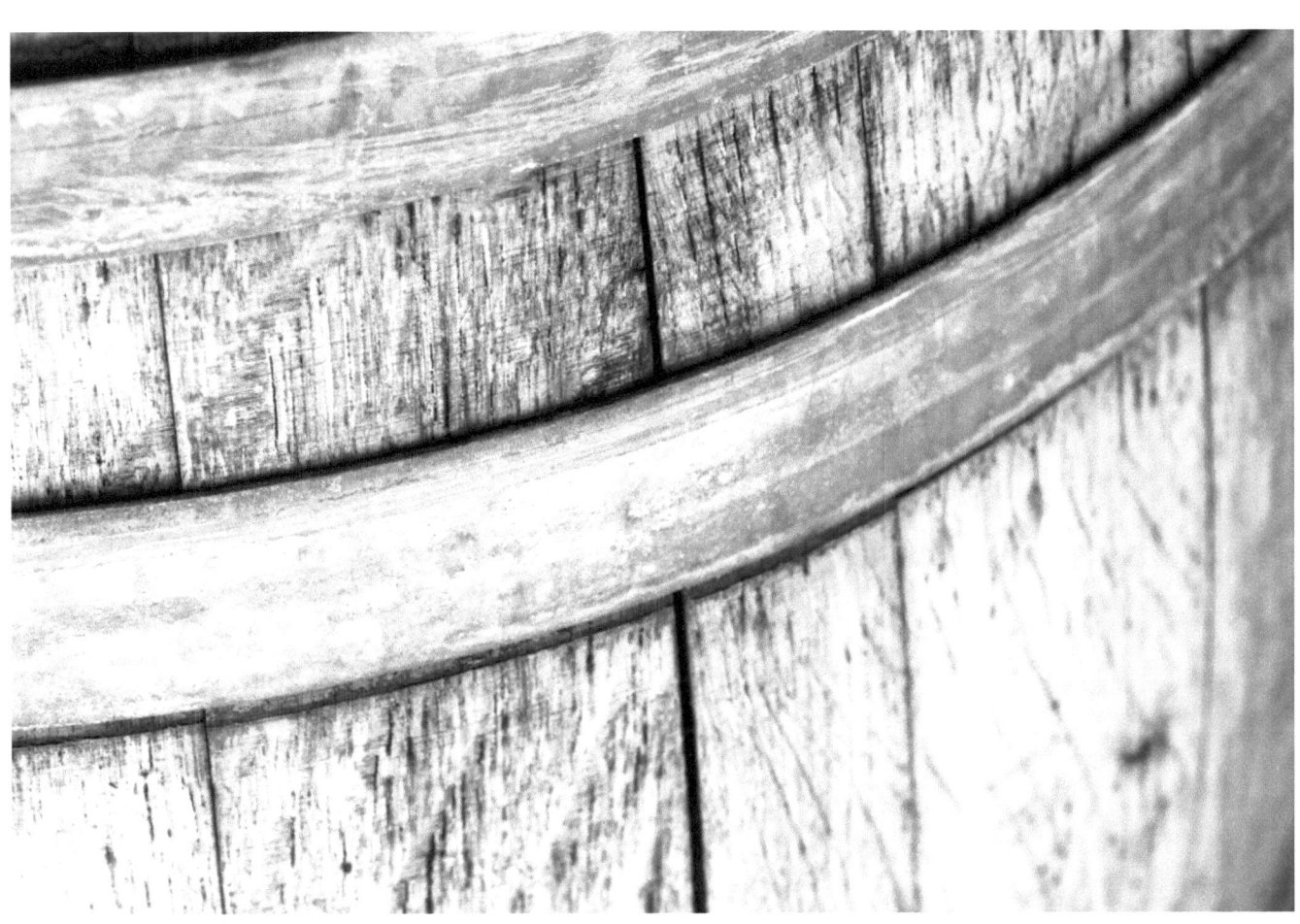

3151

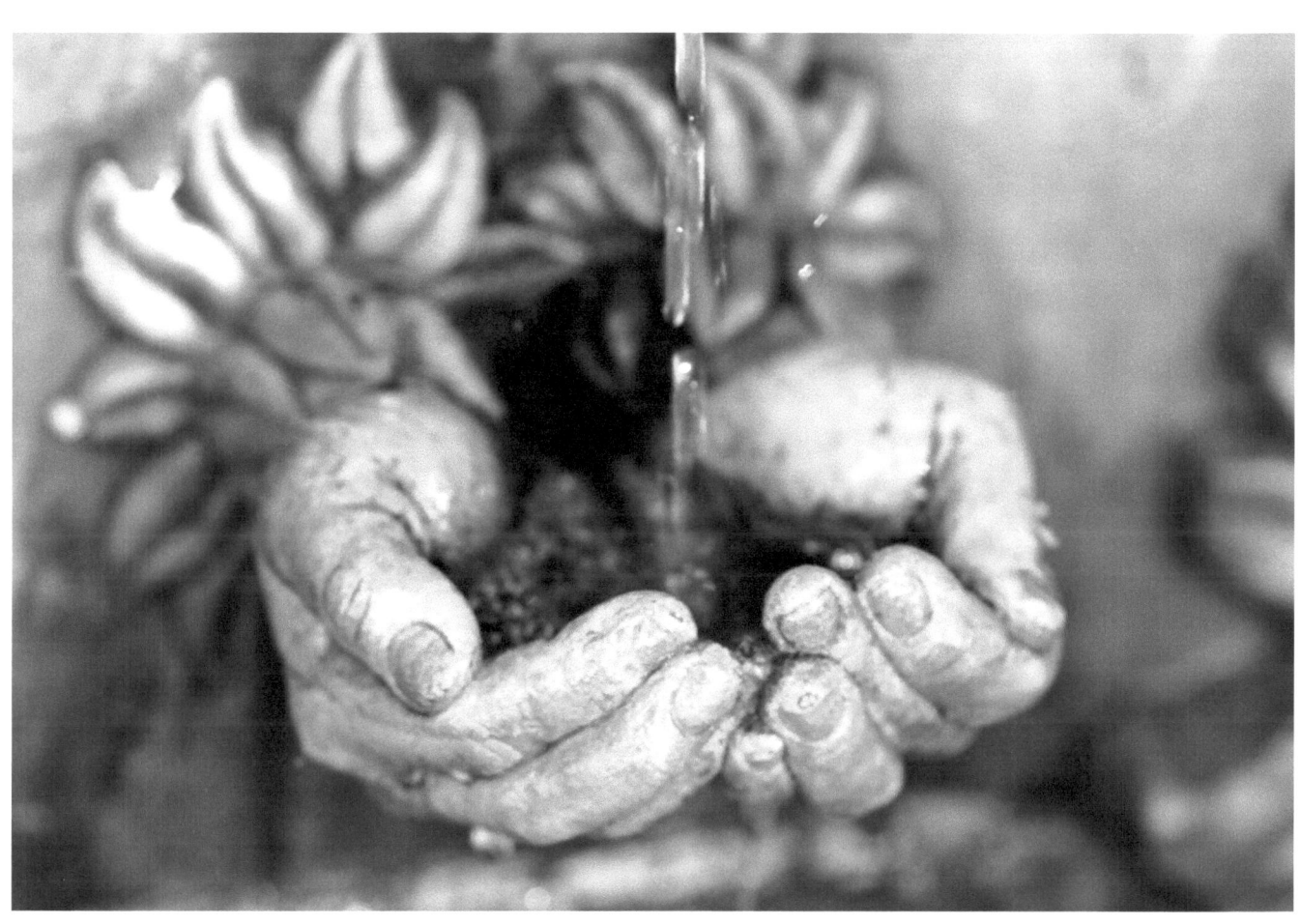

3720

.

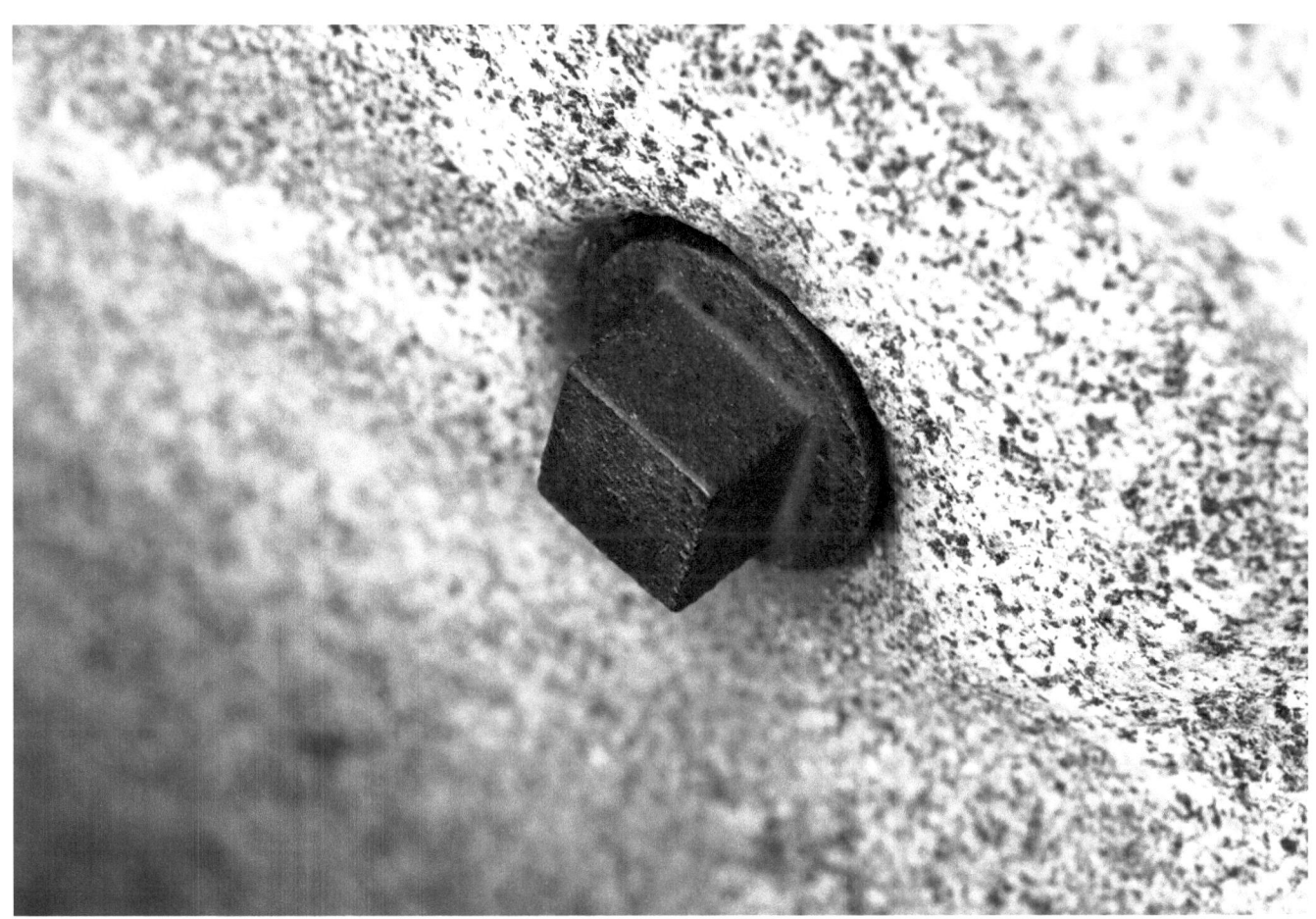

4035

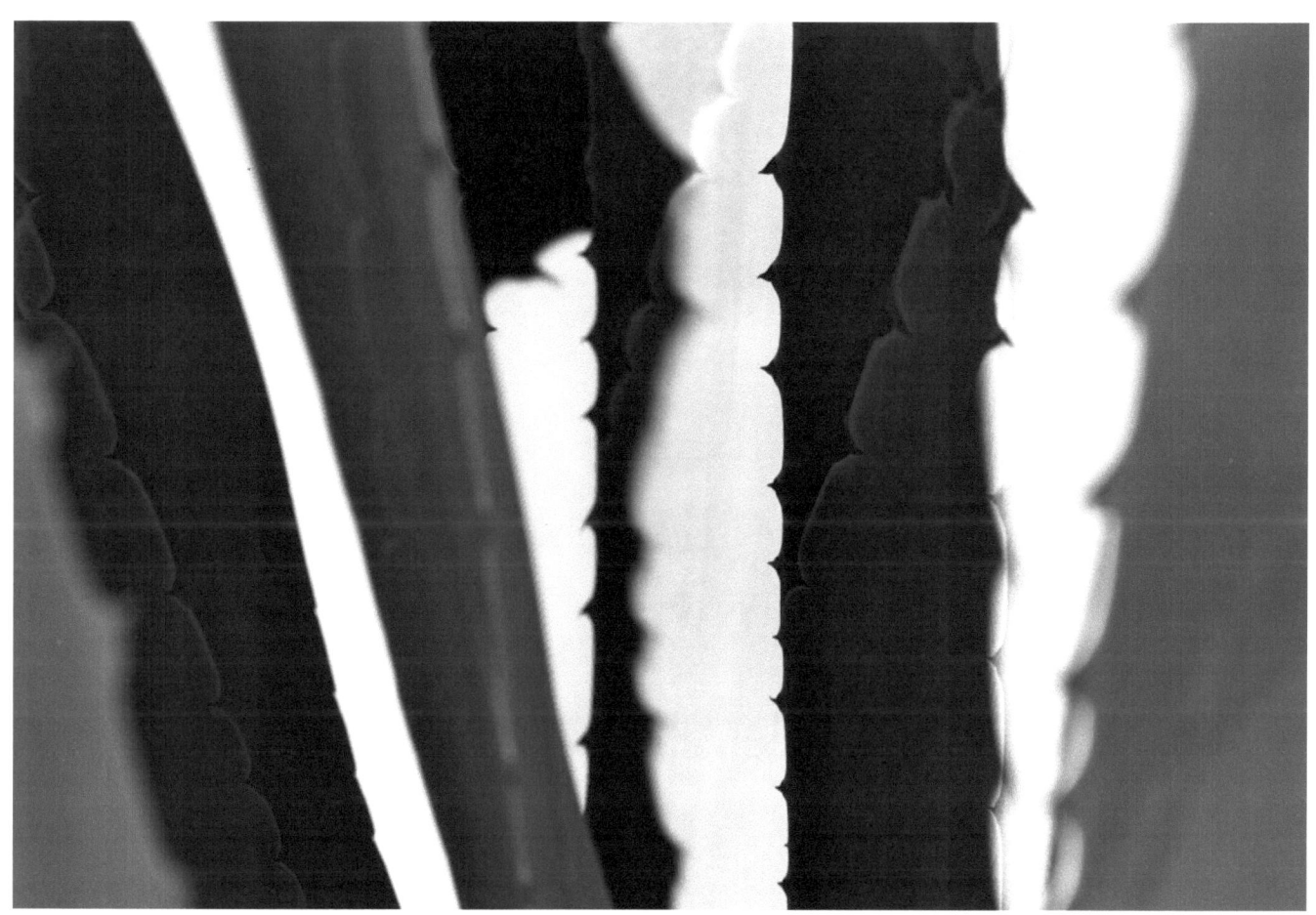

4099

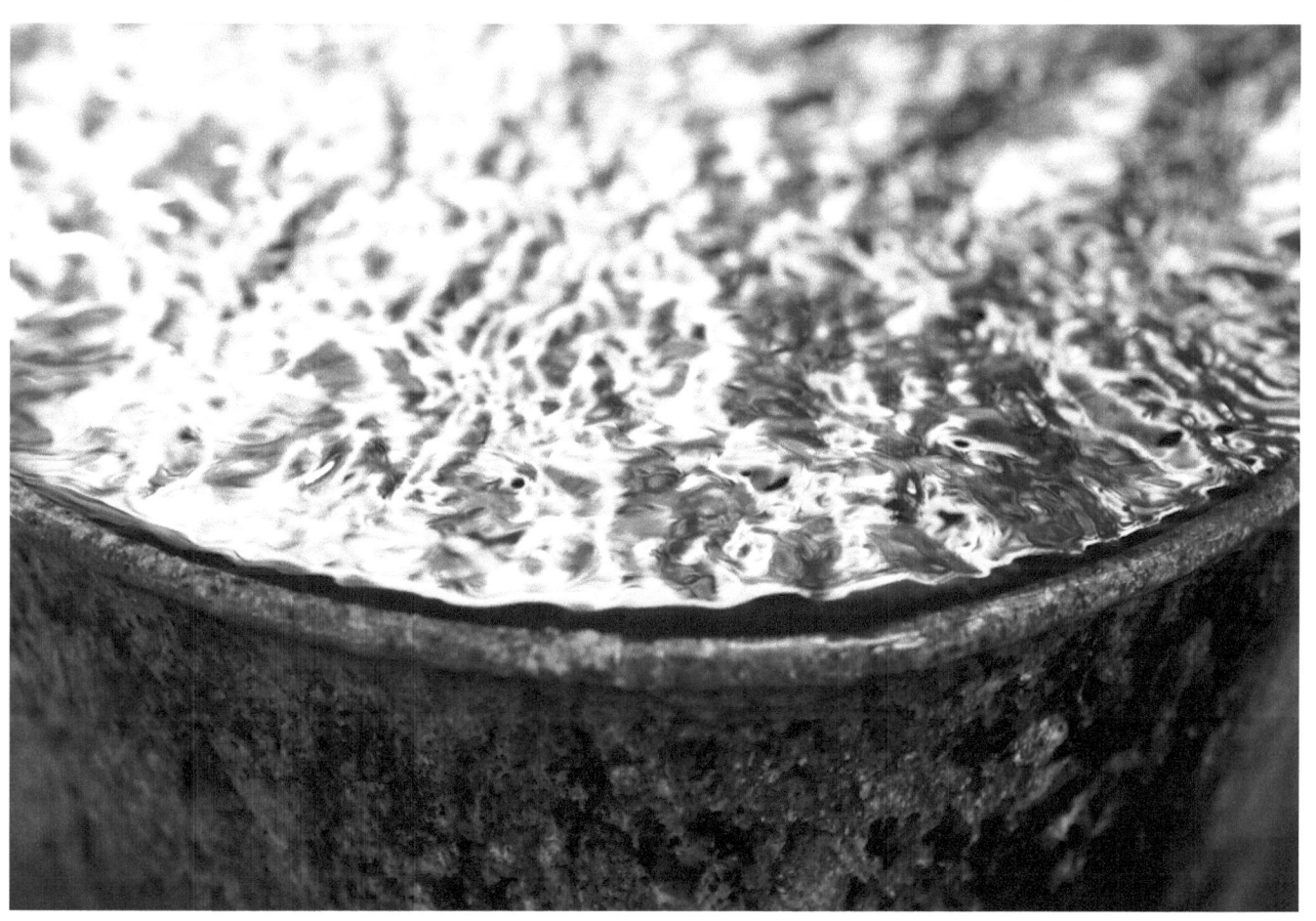

4533

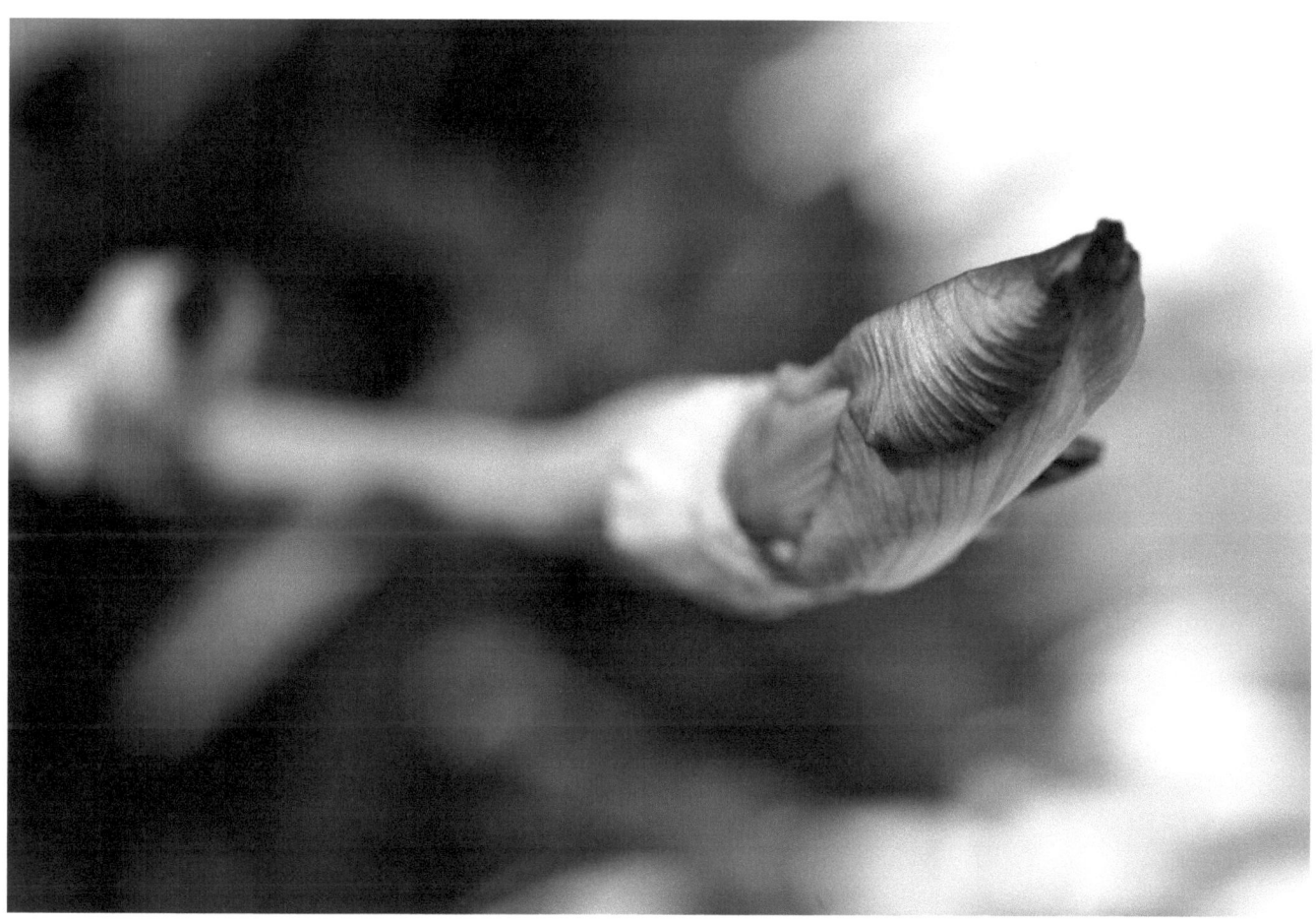

5492

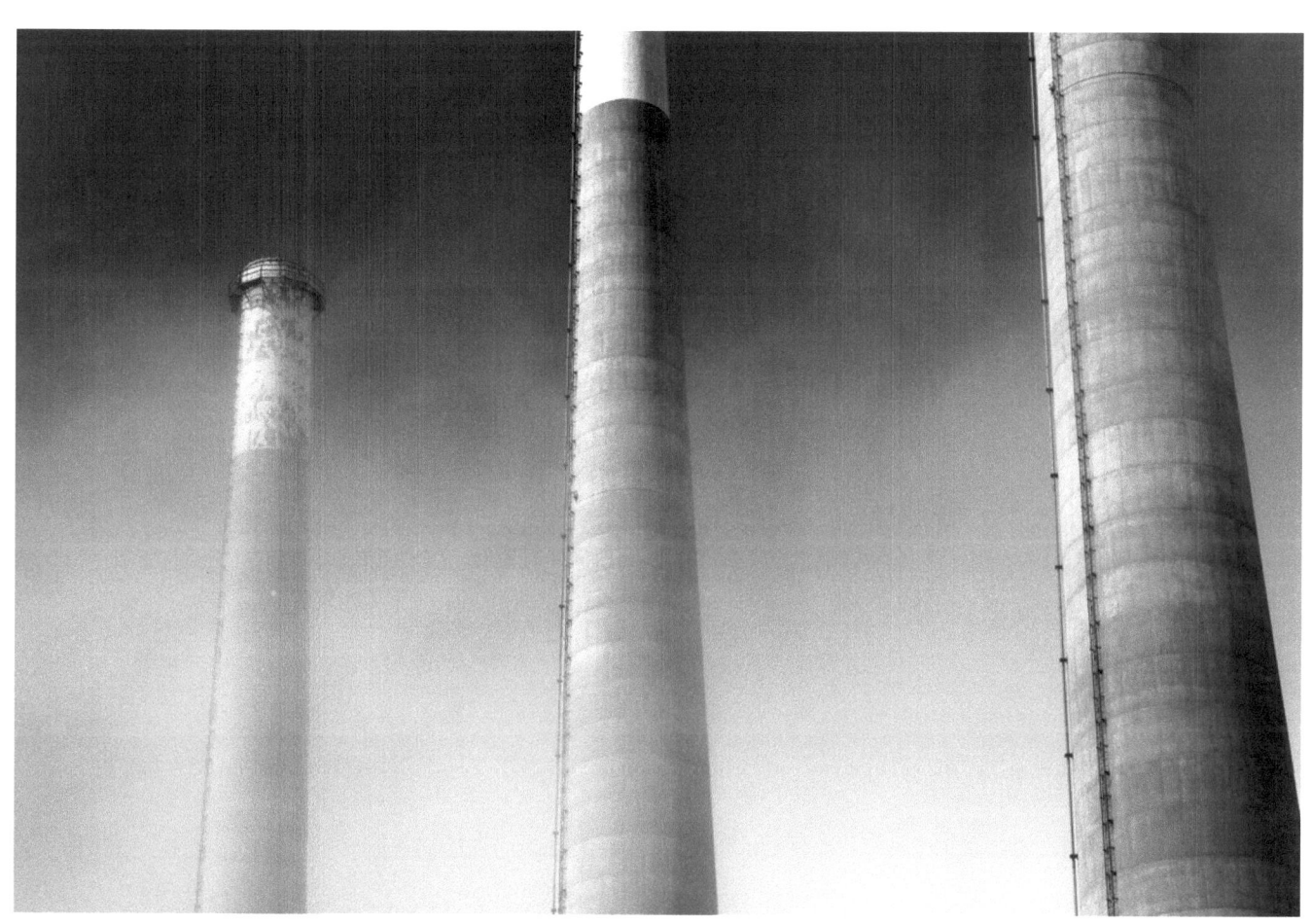

5541

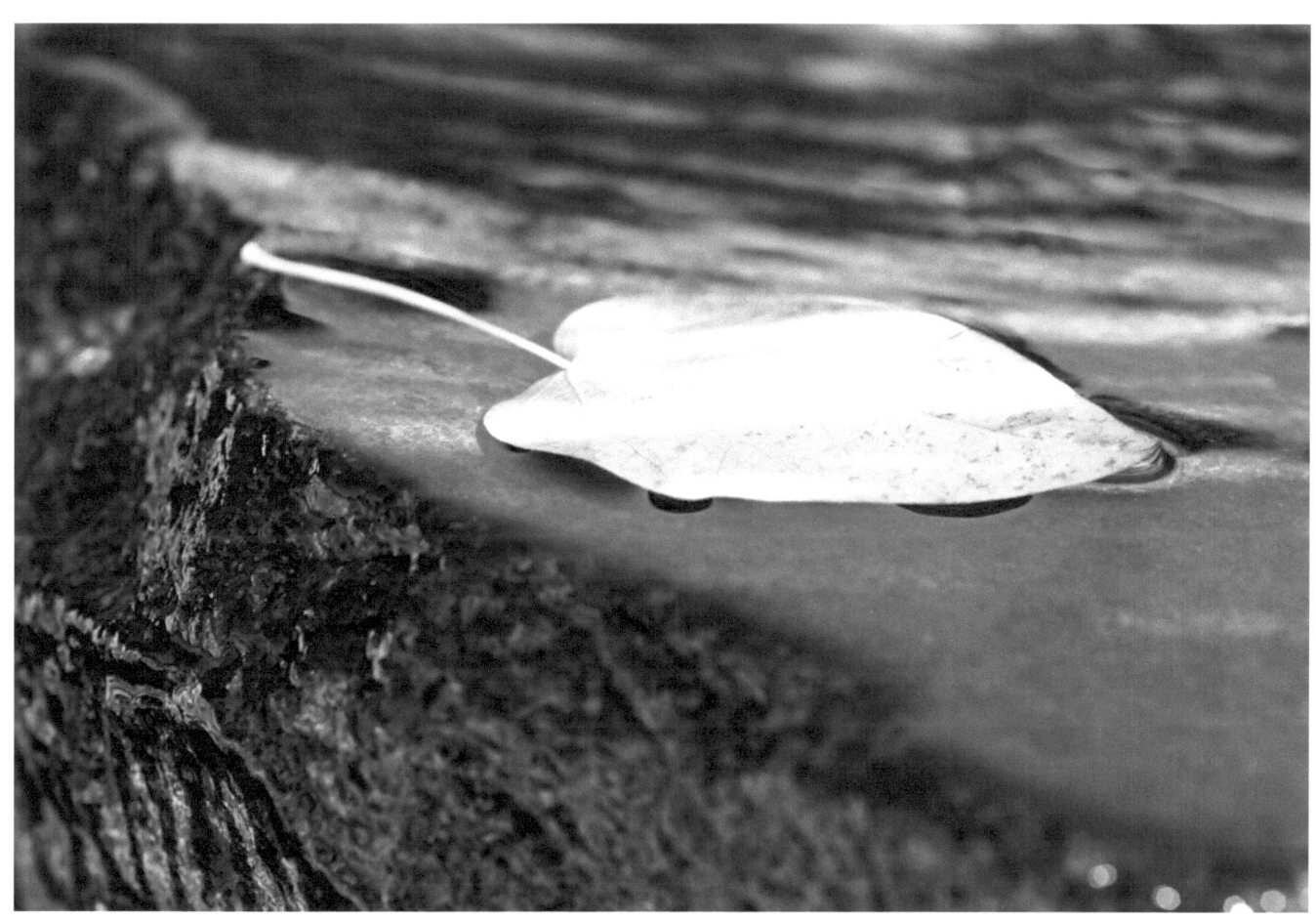

5750

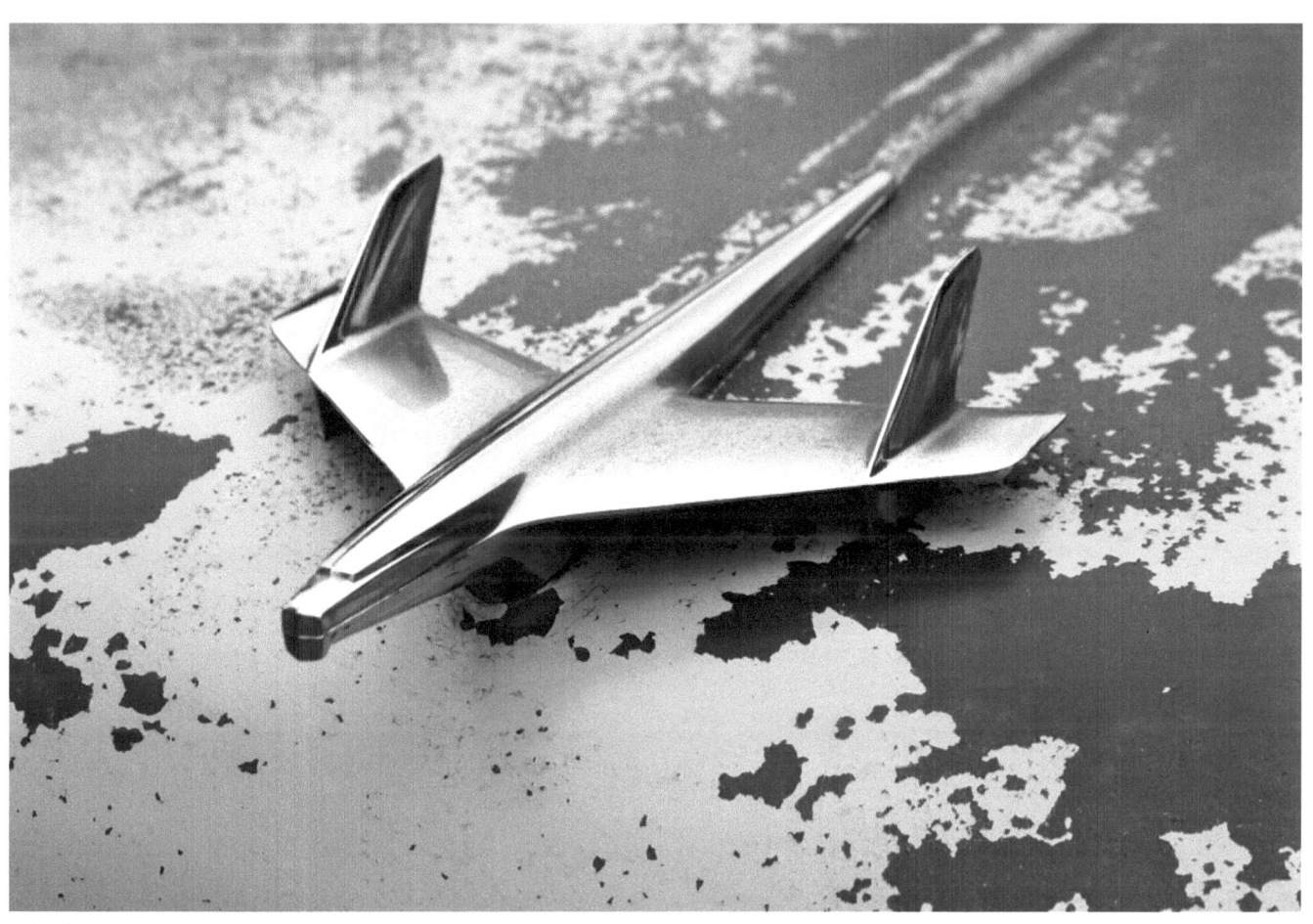

5846

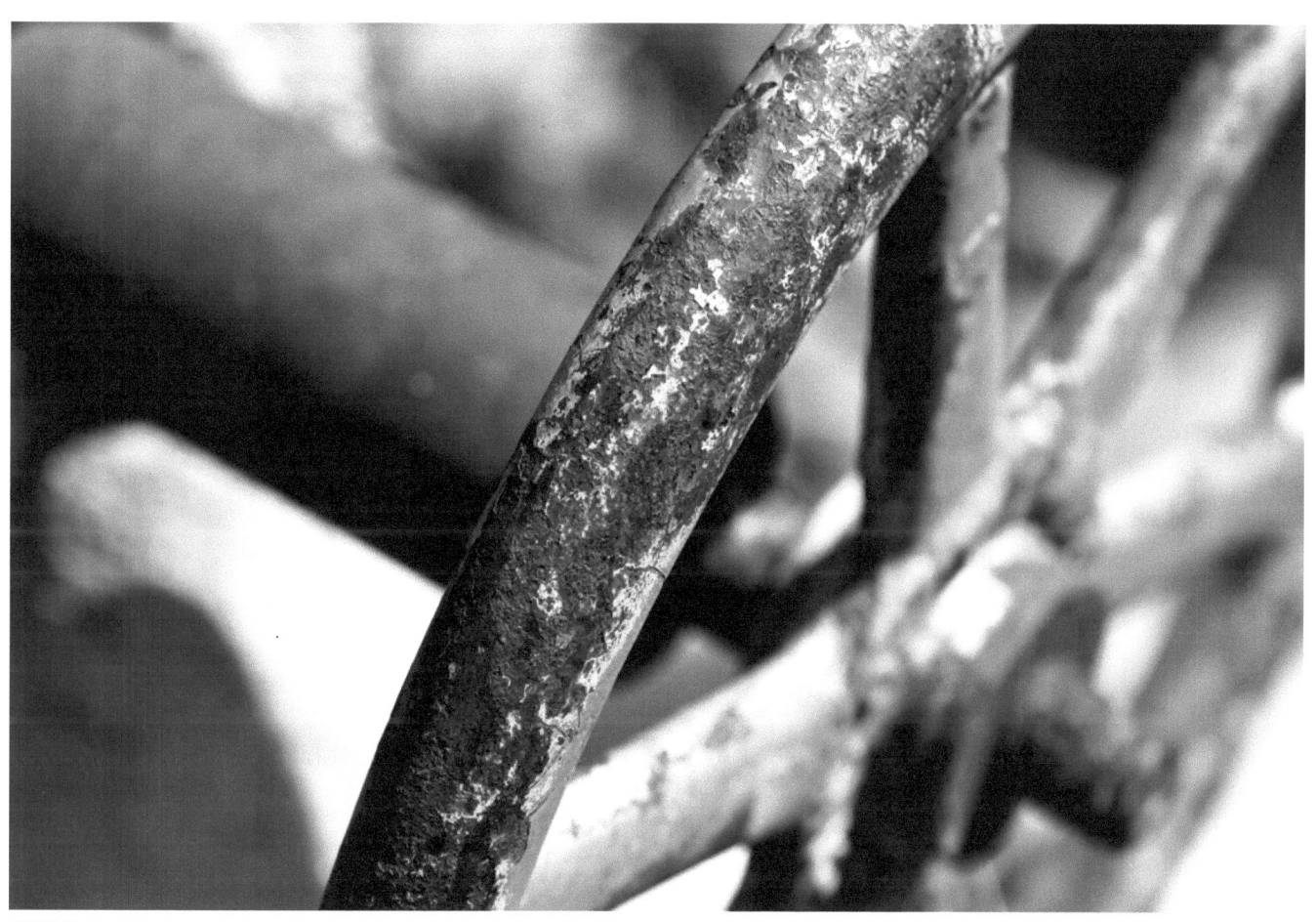

6095

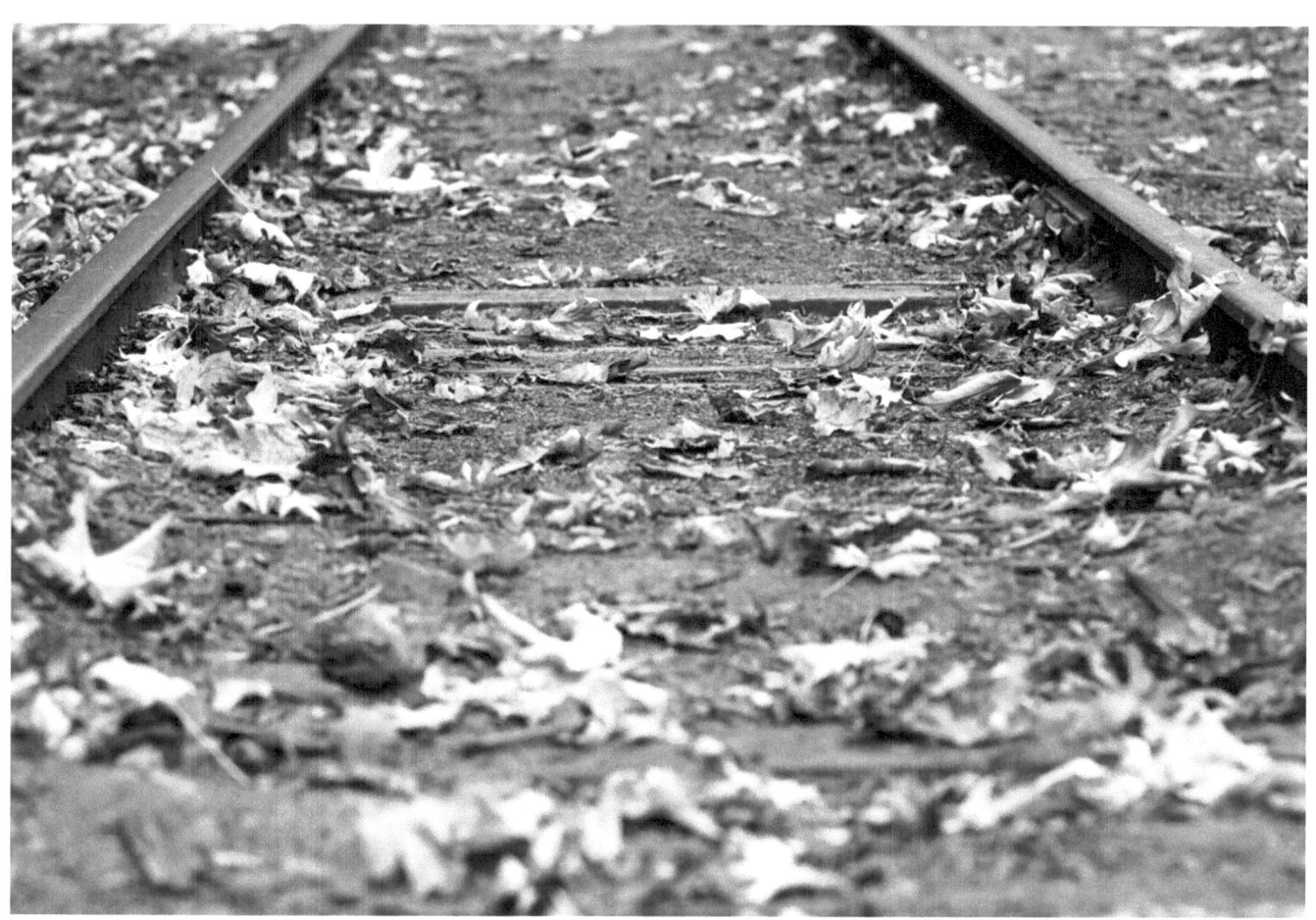

6176

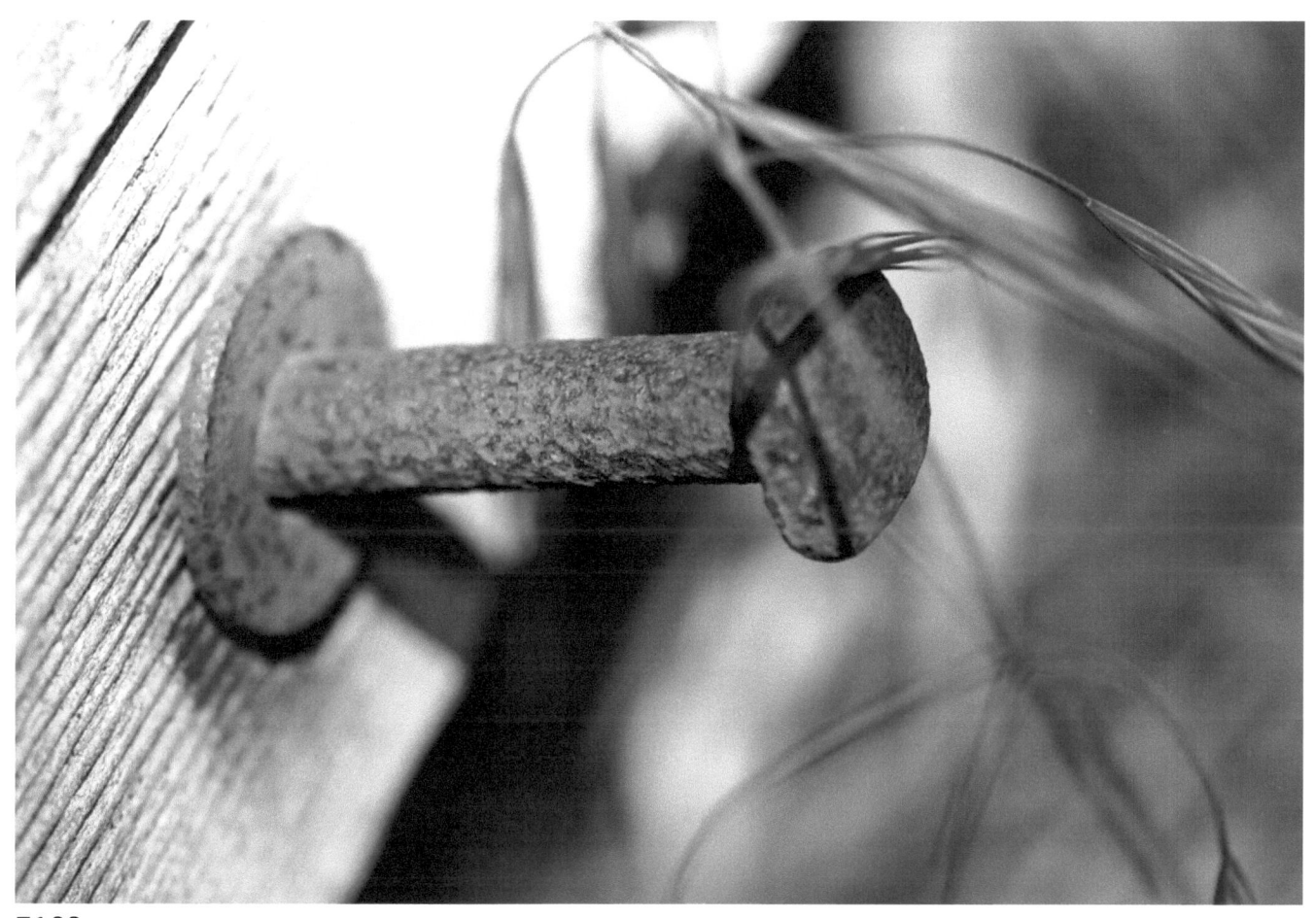

7182

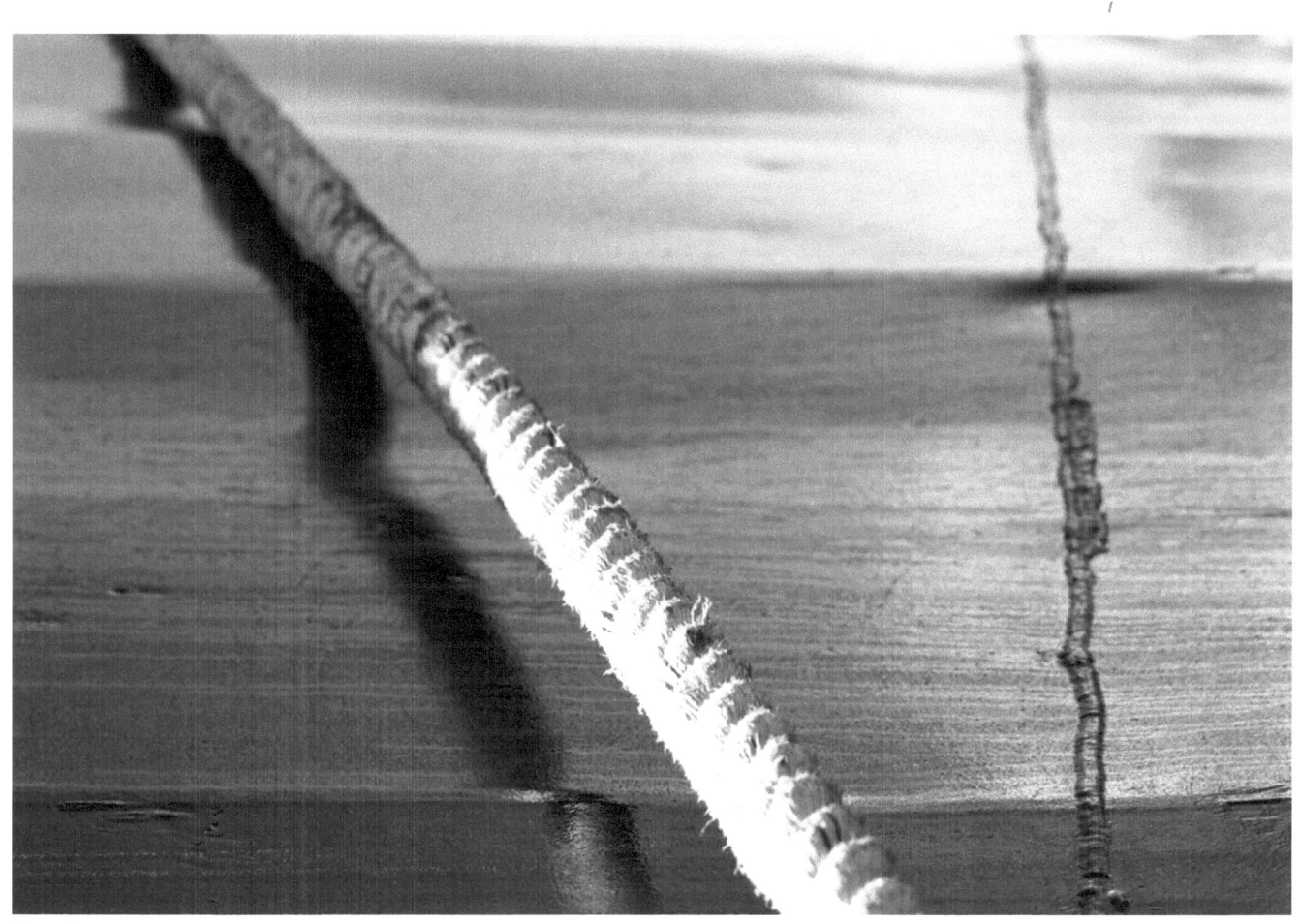

8470

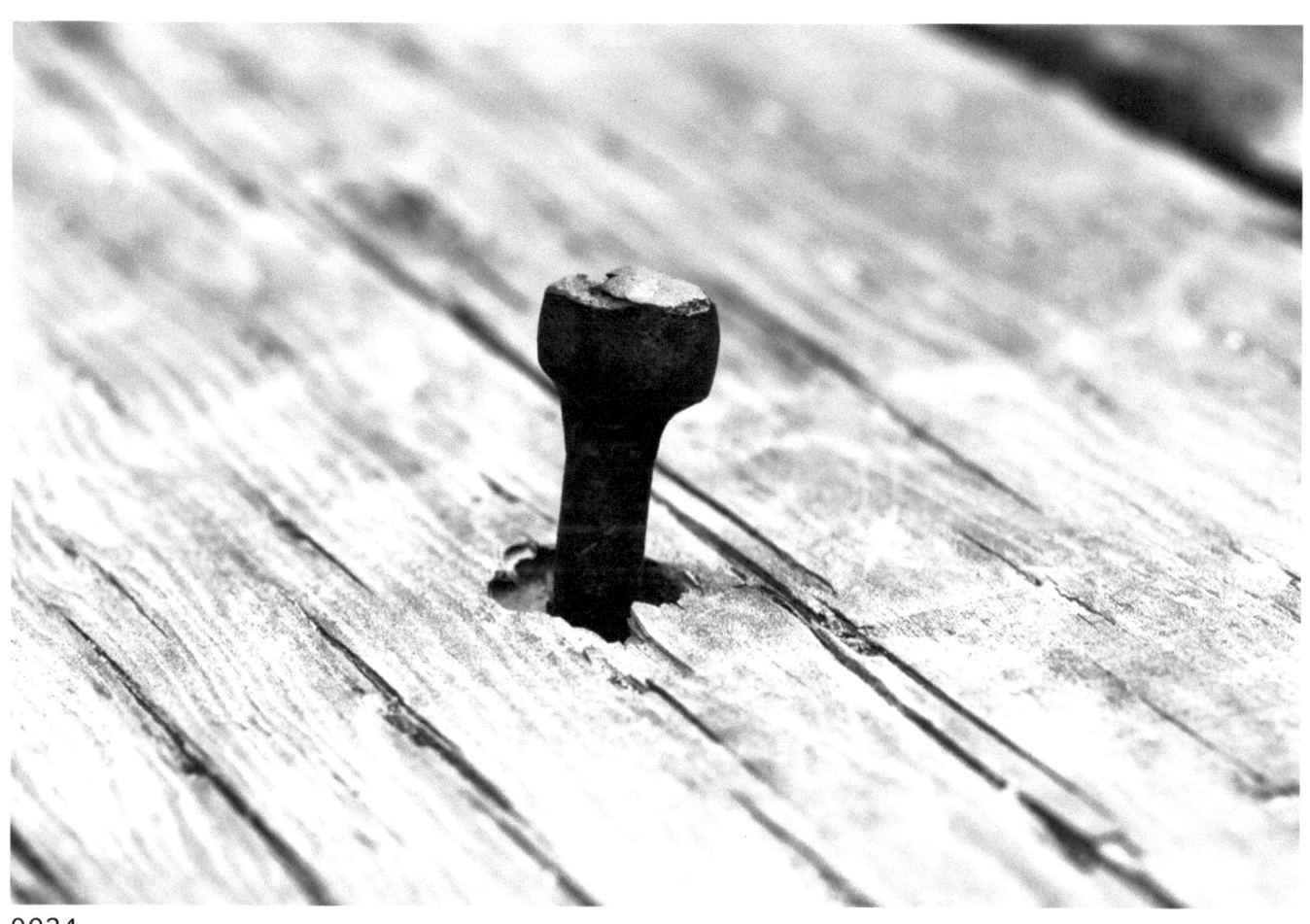

9024

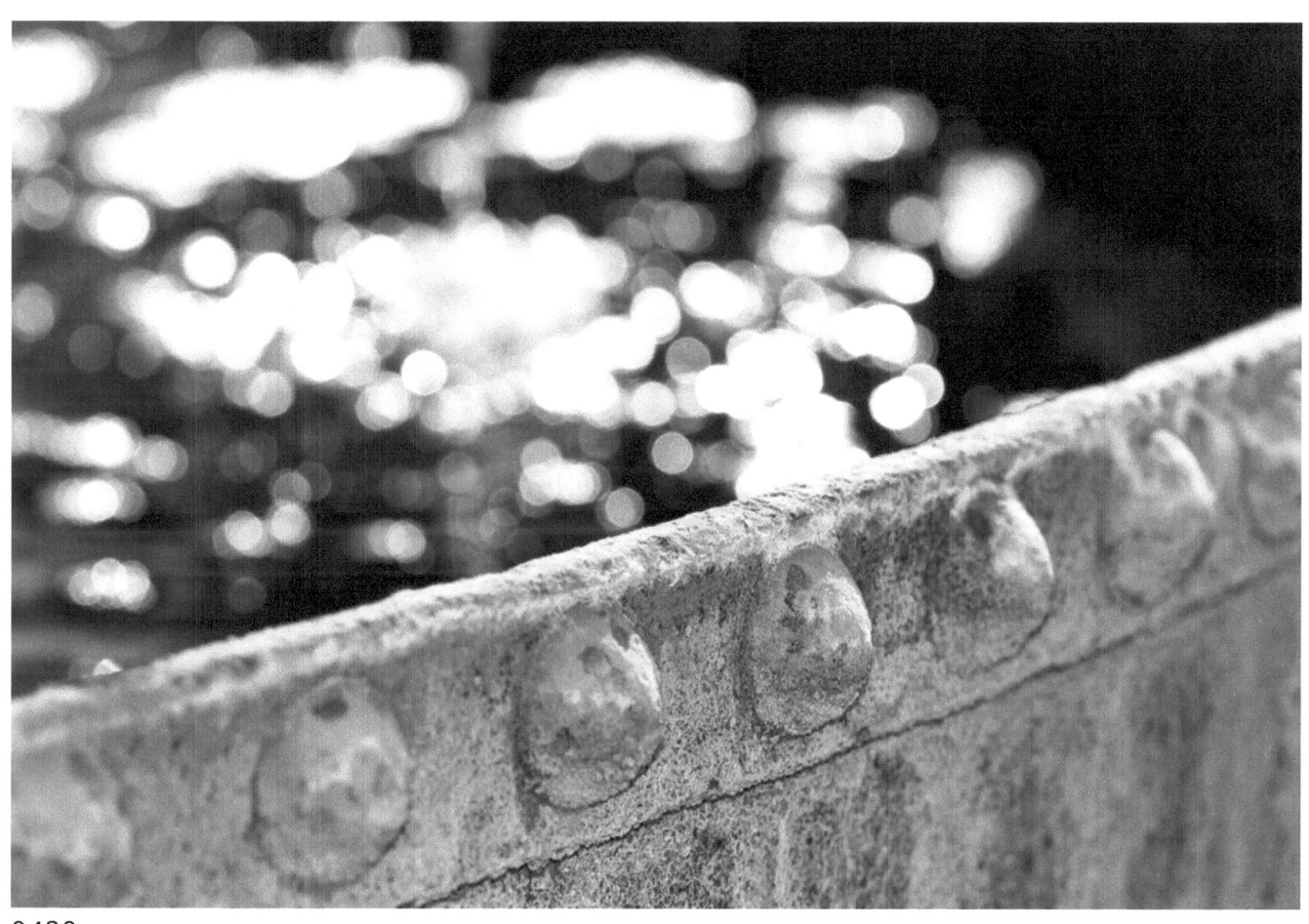

9430

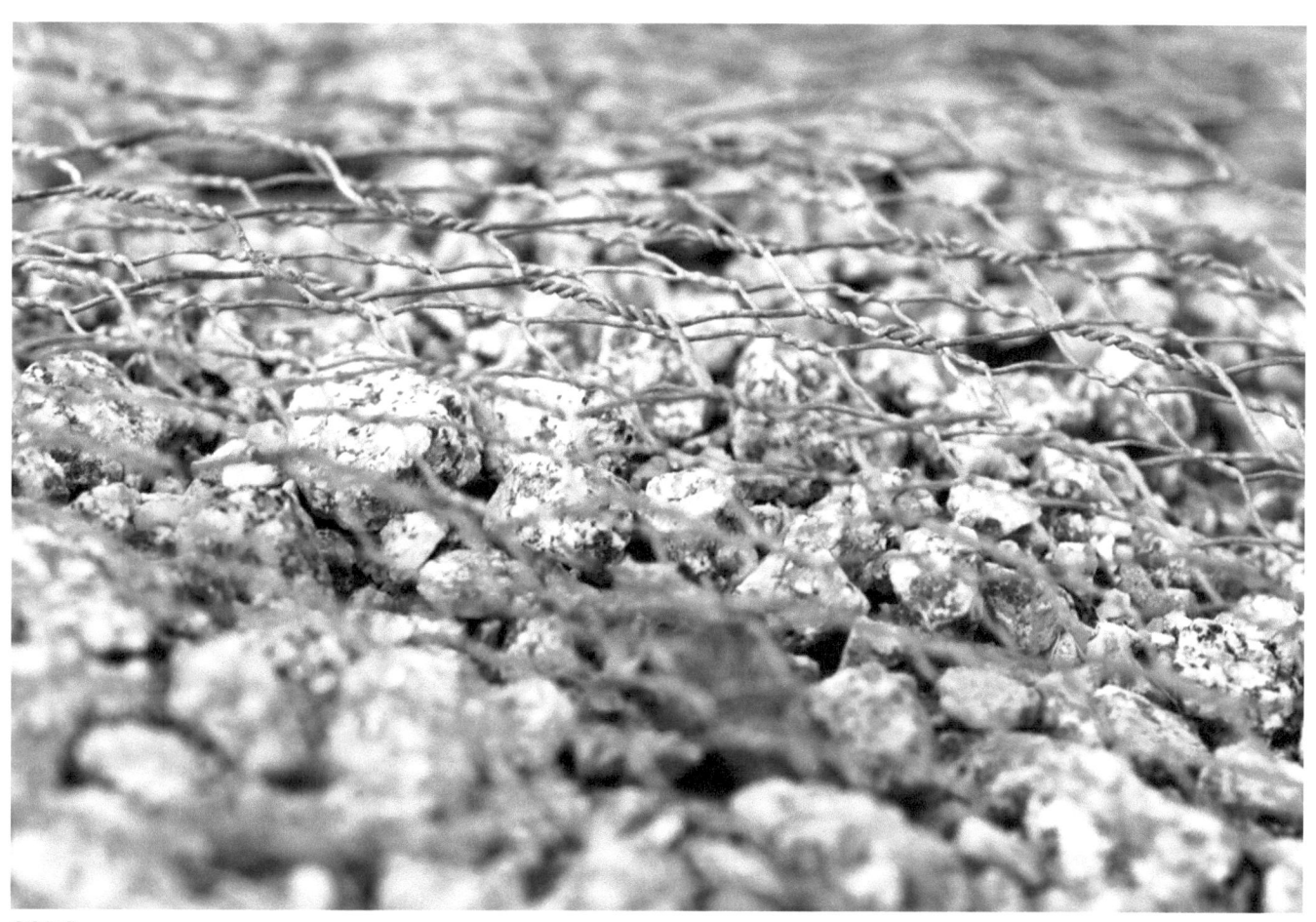

9970

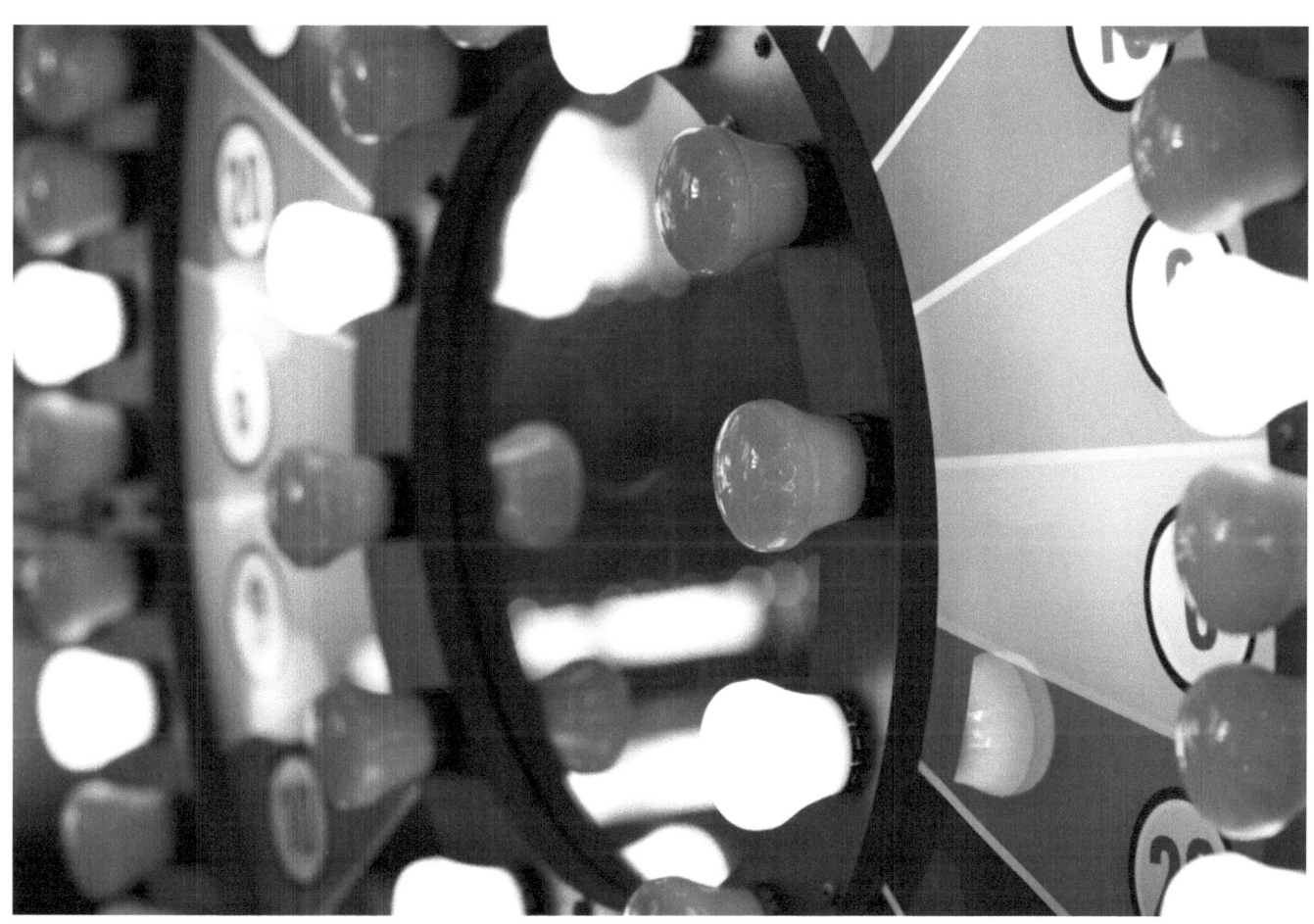

9980

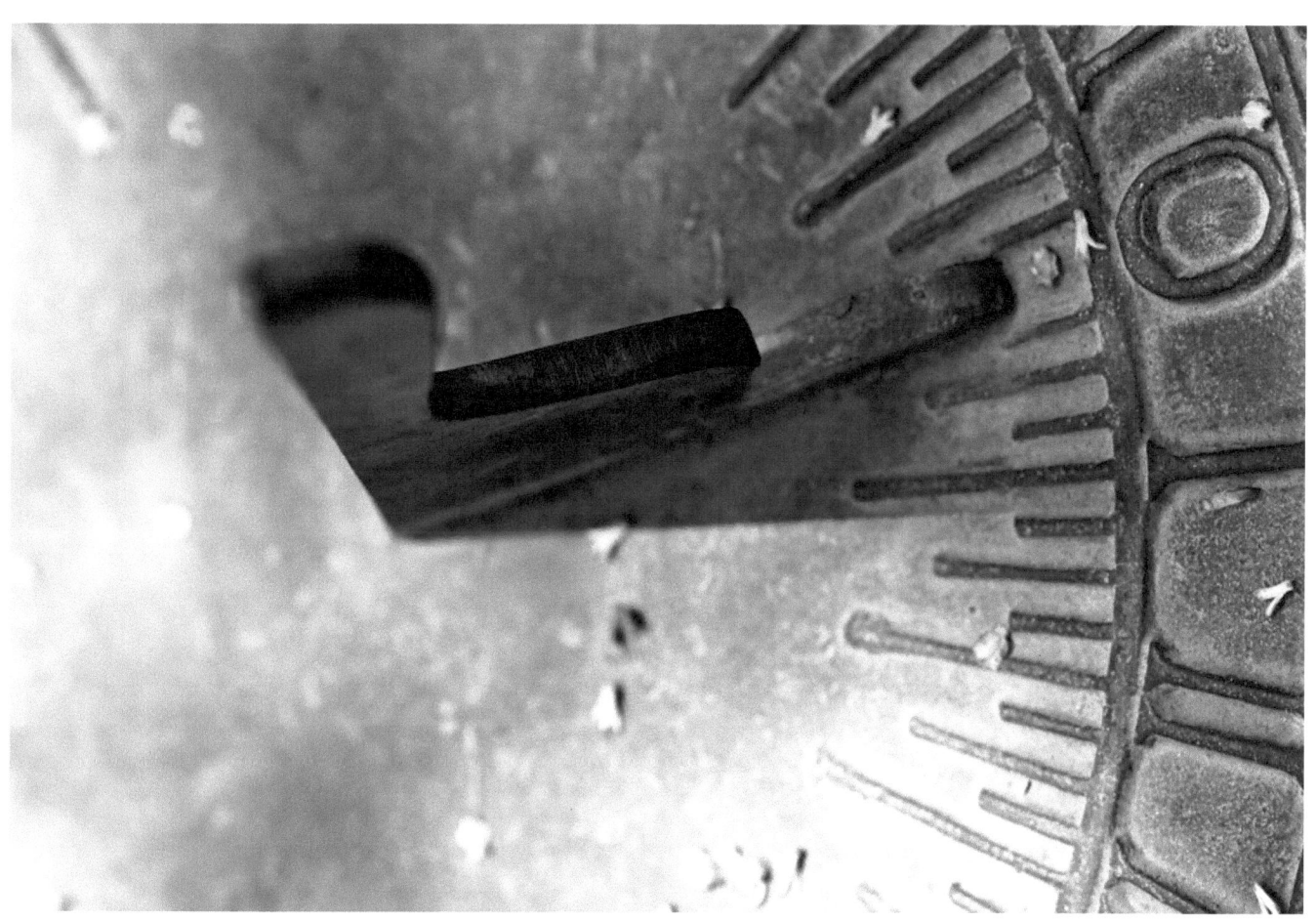

10002